PIONEERS IN HISTORY
PEOPLE WHO CARE
MICHAEL POLLARD

HEINEMANN CHILDREN'S REFERENCE
a division of Heinemann Educational Books Ltd
Halley Court, Jordan Hill, Oxford OX2 8EJ

OXFORD LONDON EDINBURGH
MELBOURNE SYDNEY AUCKLAND
MADRID ATHENS BOLOGNA
SINGAPORE IBADAN NAIROBI HARARE
GABORONE KINGSTON PORTSMOUTH NH(USA)

ISBN 0 431 00555 9

British Library Cataloguing in Publication Data
Pollard, Michael, *1931–*
    People who care.
    1. Philanthropy - Biographies - Collections
    I. Title   II. Series
361.7'4'0922

Designed by Pardoe Blacker Limited
Picture research by Faith Perkins

Printed in Hong Kong

91 92 93 94 95 10 9 8 7 6 5 4 3 2 1

Photographic credits

a = above b = below r = right l = left

The author and publishers wish to acknowledge, with
thanks, the following photographic sources:

The cover pictures are courtesy of Camera Press and
the Peabody Trust

Aspect Picture Library pp15*a*, 29*b*, 33*a*; Barnardo's
Photographic Archive pp20, 21*a* and *b*; Bettmann Archive
pp7*a* and *b*, 8, 18, 19*a* and *b*; Bridgeman Art Library pp6
(Sir John Soane's Museum), 10 (William Penn House), 11*a*
(Royal Holloway College & Bedford New College); Camera
Press pp9*b*, 39*a* and *b*, 43*a*; Colorphoto Hans Hinz p9*a*;
Comite International de la Croix-Rouge p23*b*; Mary Evans
Picture Library pp13*b*, 22, 27*a*, 34, 36; Hulton-Deutsch
Collection pp16, 31*a*; Lloyd's Register, London p26; Peter
Newark's Pictures pp17*a*, 23*a*, 24, 25*a* and *b*, 27*b*, 28, 29*a*,
35*a*; Magnum pp5*a* and *b* (F Scianna), 37*b* (W Eugene
Smith), 38 (Raghu Rai), 41*a* (Bruce Davidson), 42, 43*b*
(Gideon Mendel); Courtesy of the Peabody Trust p12;
Popperfoto p41*b*; RNIB p15*b*; Ann Ronan Picture Library
pp11*b*, 13*a*, 14; Joseph Rowntree Memorial Trust p31*b*; Save
the Children Fund pp32, 33*b*; Syndication International p4;
Topham Picture Library pp35*b*, 37*a*, 40; York City Archives
p30.

The publishers have made every effort to trace the copyright
holders, but if they have inadvertently overlooked any,
they will be pleased to make the necessary arrangements at
the first opportunity.

Note to the reader

In this book there are some words in the text which are printed in **bold** type. This shows that the word is
listed in the glossary on page 46. The glossary gives a brief explanation of words which may be new to you.

Contents

Introduction

Some peoples lives are harder and less happy than others. They may be too ill or too old to work, or have nowhere to live or no money to buy food. They may be children whose parents have died or whose families have been split up. They may be people who are **mentally ill** and find it difficult to look after themselves. They may be families caught up in war or who are starving because of **famine**. All are people who need help to improve the quality of their own lives, or even just to stay alive.

Today, some of the money people pay to governments in **taxes** is spent helping people in need. Many people also give money to organisations which provide special help in their own country and abroad. These organisations are called **charities**. Other people give up their free time to help people in their local area.

Looking after others

Many people believe that people should care for anyone who needs help. Jesus Christ told his followers that they should look after the old, the sick and the hungry. Mohammed gave the same message to followers of **Islam**. Followers of **Hinduism** and Jewish people too, as well as Sikhs and others, give money and time to help people in need.

How can enough food be provided for the world's hungry people? What can be done to find a cure for terrible diseases such as **leprosy**, cancer or AIDS? How can the lives of some poor or lonely people be improved? What is the best way to look after the disabled or mentally ill? Over the past 200 years, more and more people have worried about these kinds of problems and what can be done about them.

◀ Children of striking coal-miners in Huddersfield, England, in 1908, waiting for free soup at a kitchen set up by a group of helpers.

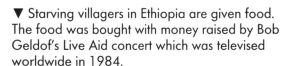

▲ In many countries today, people without work or food have to beg in the streets.

Finding the answers

This book is about women and men who have asked questions like this and have spent their lives trying to find answers. Some, like Clara Barton and Henri Dunant, worked directly with the victims of war or a peacetime disaster such as an earthquake. Others, like Johann Pestalozzi, tried out new ideas and then wrote about them. They are all people who have made life better for millions of people, including the mentally or physically ill or disabled people, prisoners, children without homes and soldiers wounded in battle. People who care in this way are called **humanitarians**.

People in this book, like Seerbohm Rowntree, also tried to ask the question, *Why?* Why are some people in the world hungry, when there is enough food for everybody? Why are some people poor and without jobs, when there is work to be done? Some people now think they have found the answers to these questions, but that governments will not listen to them.

Introduction

This book tells the stories of some of the people who have worked to make life better for other people. Without them, life would have been much harder for millions of people. However, for millions of other people life is still hard. Humanitarian work now goes on all over the world. Some of the organisations you will read about, such as the Red Cross or Save the Children, are still at work, and many new ones such as Band Aid have been set up. Governments in wealthy countries such as Britain and the United States send some help to people in poorer countries. Many young people spend a year or two in other countries working with caring organisations such as Voluntary Service Overseas or the Peace Corps before they start their own careers. In spite of all these efforts, the world is still divided into the people who 'have' and the people who 'have not', and the questions *why?* and *how?* have not yet been answered.

▼ Starving villagers in Ethiopia are given food. The food was bought with money raised by Bob Geldof's Live Aid concert which was televised worldwide in 1984.

Philippe Pinel

Many people who suffer from mental illness behave in ways which are hard to understand. Some mentally ill people cannot do ordinary everyday things like finding their way about. Others are frightened to go out.

Until about 200 years ago, people with mental illnesses were treated very badly. Many people believed that mental illness was caused by the devil or by witchcraft. Mentally ill people were given no treatment to help them get better or to live a more normal life. They were kept in special hospitals called **asylums**. The word asylum means a place of peace and safety, but these asylums were far from that. Patients were given only just enough food to keep them alive, and they were left with nothing to do all day. They were chained up to stop them escaping, because they were thought to be dangerous.

People used to visit asylums as a form of entertainment. They would laugh at the patients and tease them to make them behave oddly. Crowds went to asylums like Bedlam in London and the Lunatics Tower in Vienna for an enjoyable day out.

Taking off the chains

Philippe Pinel was a French doctor who believed that it was wrong to treat mental patients in this way. In 1791 he wrote a report saying that many patients would get better if they were treated properly. In 1792 Pinel was put in charge of an asylum where he was able to try out his ideas.

He ordered the chains to be taken off all mentally ill patients. They were to be treated with kindness, given good food and allowed to walk about in the fresh air. When the patients no longer struggled to free themselves from their chains, they became much calmer, and better food and cleaner surroundings improved their general health.

◀ Bedlam, one of London's asylums, over 200 years ago. The well-dressed visitors in the background have come sightseeing. The name 'Bedlam' is a short form of Bethlehem, the hospital's real name. Now the word 'bedlam' means loud, noisy chaos, which tells us what the asylum must have been like.

▶ Pinel orders the chains to be removed from patients at the Bicetre asylum in Paris.

The spread of Pinel's ideas

Many doctors could not believe that it was safe to leave patients unchained, but soon everyone who heard Pinel's ideas was talking about what he had achieved. One of the visitors who came to visit Pinel to learn about his work was an American doctor called Benjamin Rush. Rush was so impressed with what he saw that when he returned to the United States he arranged for mentally ill patients in his home state of Pennsylvania to be unchained.

Dorothea Dix, an American teacher, also became interested in Pinel's ideas, and in 1841 she too began to work for better treatment of mental patients. Dix persuaded the people in charge of more than 30 hospitals in the United States to change to Pinel's methods. She also travelled in Europe, spreading Pinel's ideas and working to improve conditions for mentally ill patients.

Philippe Pinel, Dorothea Dix and others made life better for mentally ill people, but there was still a long way to go. Patients were no longer chained, but they were still locked up. Today, doctors understand more about mental illness, and many patients are helped so much that they are able to leave hospital and live and work in the community.

▼ Dorothea Dix was a teacher and nurse who became interested in mental illness. Her work improved life for mentally ill patients in the United States and Europe.

7

Johann Pestalozzi

▲ Johann Pestalozzi believed that learning should be interesting to children.

Today, in almost every country of the world, all children go to school for at least a few years. The education they are given at school is intended to help them to make up their own minds about the world. Teachers now believe that it is important for children to think and to find things out for themselves, and this is why there is so much 'finding out' in school.

Two hundred years ago, children's lives were very different. Usually, only the sons of rich families went to school. The girls stayed at home and learned to cook and sew and how to look after a house and a family. The children of poor families were sent out to work as soon as they could do anything useful. Children as young as three or four had to work in the fields scaring birds off the crops. By the age of eight, many boys and girls worked long hours in mines or factories.

A Swiss man, Johann Pestalozzi, thought that it was unfair that only the sons of wealthy families went to school. He believed that all children should be given the chance to learn about the world they lived in.

Learning about teaching

In the 1700s, schools were often unhappy places, where teachers shouted at the children and beat them if they did not learn fast enough. Lessons were boring lists of facts. Teachers never explained anything.

Pestalozzi thought that this was the wrong way to teach. In 1769, when he was 23, he started his own school at Yverdon in Switzerland. The school's pupils were children who had no homes. Pestalozzi wanted to find out how children learned, so that he could decide on the best way to teach them. He found that the children in his school learned more if they were treated kindly, and if they understood what they were being taught. The best way to teach was to start with things the children already knew about, and then to go on to new and different ideas.

Most important of all, Pestalozzi discovered that it did not matter what kind of family children came from. All children seemed to learn equally well, girls as well as boys.

Schools for all

For people interested in education these were exciting new ideas. In 1801 Pestalozzi wrote a book about teaching, called *How Gertrude teaches her children*, and many visitors came to his school from other countries to see him at work. He died in 1827, but his ideas were not forgotten.

Teachers such as the German Friedrich Froebel and the Italian Maria Montessori followed his ideas and took them further in their own work. Pestalozzi's ideas are still used in schools today. When young children find out about water, sand and clay by playing with them, they are learning in the way that Pestalozzi first suggested.

▼ The children in Pestalozzi's schools had nowhere else to live. Pestalozzi acted as their father as well as their teacher.

▲ Learning through activities was one of Pestalozzi's ideas which is still used in schools today.

Elizabeth Fry

One day in February 1813 a visitor went to Newgate Prison in London. A friend had asked her to go to the prison to see the women prisoners there. The visitor's name was Elizabeth Fry.

Fry was shocked by what she saw. More than 300 prisoners were crowded together in one room. They had to sleep on the floor without blankets or bedding. Prisoners who were ill were left among the others, with no doctor or nurse to attend to them. Many of the women were dressed only in rags, and were freezing cold. There was no heat or light, and so little food that the prisoners often fought for it.

All kinds of prisoners lived together. Some were murderers, while others had been sent to prison for small crimes such as stealing a loaf of bread. Some prisoners would be there for the rest of their lives. Others would be freed after a few months. Women took their children to prison with them or had babies while they were there.

Better prisons

Nearly 200 years ago, most people were not concerned about conditions in prisons. They thought that prison was meant to be a punishment, and that therefore it should be unpleasant.

Unlike most people, Elizabeth Fry believed that there was some good in everyone, and that no one should be forced to live in such terrible conditions. However, it was not easy to interest anyone in the idea that prisoners should be better treated.

Fry collected a group of friends together and they began to work for better conditions for women in Newgate Prison. They helped the women prisoners by taking in clothes and food for them. Elizabeth Fry encouraged the prisoners to learn skills such as sewing, so that they were able to make goods which were sold to bring them some money. Fry helped the women to organise their lives in prison and with their agreement she started a school for the children. These changes improved the lives of the Newgate prisoners and their children, but Elizabeth Fry knew that other changes were needed. Only the government could pass laws which would improve the lives of all prisoners.

▼ Elizabeth Fry was a Quaker. Quakers are Christians who believe that it is important to help and to care for other people. 'Plain' Quakers like Elizabeth Fry wore very simple clothes.

► Newgate Prison in London, where Elizabeth Fry first saw the terrible conditions in which women prisoners were kept.

Changing peoples minds

In 1818, Elizabeth Fry was asked to give evidence to Parliament on the conditions in the country's prisons. She was the first woman to advise a government. Elizabeth Fry invited members of Parliament to visit Newgate with her to see how bad conditions were, and in 1824 the government minister in charge of prisons, Sir Robert Peel, made some of the changes that she wanted. From then on, women in the larger prisons were housed separately from the men and had women guards. Following Elizabeth Fry's ideas, women prisoners were given useful work to do and were taught to read. Teams of visitors were organised to inspect the prisons and to report on conditions in them. This meant that not only were the changes made, but people were given the job of making sure they were carried out.

Elizabeth Fry carried on with her work of forming groups of women to visit and make friends with women prisoners, and she spent the last years of her life travelling through Europe. She talked to many people, giving lectures and spreading her ideas. Elizabeth Fry died in 1845. Her care and concern for prisoners had brought about the beginning of change in the way people thought about prisons, and in the way prisoners were treated.

▼ Some prisoners were sent to prison on ships. These prison ships were even dirtier and more crowded than prisons on land. This ship, the *Warrior*, held 600 prisoners.

George Peabody

◄ George Peabody came to live in London in 1837, and a few years later he decided to stay there for the rest of his life.

George Peabody was born in 1795 in Danvers, a small town in Massachusetts, in the north-eastern United States. His first job was in a grocery store, and when he was about 18 he and a friend opened a shop of their own. Working hard, they built up a successful business and became very wealthy. In 1830 the friend retired, leaving George Peabody in charge of the business.

Peabody began to look around for something new to do. He decided to move to Britain and in 1837 he opened an office in London. He became a **merchant** and a banker, trading in goods brought into Britain from the United States. This business

was as successful as Peabody's earlier one, and he became the best-known American in London. He liked living in Britain and settled down to spend the rest of his life there.

Money for education

George Peabody believed very strongly that all young people should have the chance to be educated. He gave large sums of money for education in the United States. He built schools in the towns of many southern states including his home town of Danvers, which is now named Peabody after him. In 1866 he gave a great

▲ A street in central London about 120 years ago. Houses were often small and crowded together.

George Peabody

Many Londoners still live in Peabody Dwellings. The buildings look old-fashioned today, but they were a great improvement on the homes which working people had lived in. The buildings were arranged in blocks around a courtyard so that each room had light and air, and the courtyard provided a safe place for children to play. Each home had a balcony which was open to the air so that clothes could be dried on it, and each block had a laundry in the basement.

Before George Peabody died in 1869, he made sure that his work would go on after his death. By 1900, Peabody Dwellings had provided 5000 homes for Londoners. George Peabody had shown that good, healthy housing could be built for rents that ordinary people could afford to pay. In London and in other British cities, people followed his ideas. They began to clear **slum housing** and to build better homes for working people.

deal of money to provide schools for black children, because he wanted to give them a chance of education. At Baltimore in Maryland, Peabody built an art gallery, a library and a music college. At Harvard, the oldest American university, he **founded** a museum of history, and at Yale he founded a science school.

Homes for Londoners

One of the great problems of London in the middle of the 1800s was the shortage of homes for working people. Houses had too little light and air, and no water, bathrooms or **sanitation**. George Peabody believed it was wrong that people should have to live in these unhealthy conditions, and in 1862 he gave £500 000, a huge amount for those days, to build blocks of apartments which were called Peabody Dwellings.

▼ An architect's drawing of a group of Peabody Dwellings in London. They were not quite as pleasant and spacious as they look here, but they were a great improvement on the slums.

13

Louis Braille

▲ Louis Braille invented an alphabet that has helped blind people all over the world.

Louis Braille understood very well the difficulties that blind people have. He lost his sight in an accident in 1812 when he was only three years old. Braille could remember from his early years what his family and his home looked like, but as he grew older and wanted to find out more about the world, he was angry because he could not find out from books. Life is difficult for blind people in all kinds of ways, but one of the greatest problems is being unable to read printed books and newspapers.

Braille lived in France, near Paris, and when he was ten he went to the Paris School for the Blind. He was good at music, and learned to play the organ and the cello, but he went on thinking about all the things that he and other blind people could never learn, because they could neither read nor write.

Reading by touch

A number of inventors had tried to make alphabets which blind people could 'read' by touch. Alphabets like these used ordinary letters which stood out from the surface of the paper. These alphabets were not easy to use because some of the letters, such as C and G, felt very similar. Louis Braille found a better system. He worked on a way of making patterns of raised dots instead of letters.

Braille stayed on at the School for the Blind as a teacher, and in 1829, when he was 20, he published his alphabet. He showed that he was able to 'read' by moving his fingers over the dots, and to 'write', using a blunt spike to make the patterns in the paper. This alphabet could also be used to read or to write music. This made it especially interesting to Braille because of his interest in music.

Braille's new alphabet took some time to be accepted. Many people still preferred the idea of a raised alphabet of ordinary letters. It was not until 1854, two years after Braille died, that his alphabet, named Braille after him, was taught to blind people in France.

Braille by machine

Writing Braille by hand was a slow process. It was only when the typewriter and fast printing machines were invented later in the 1800s that Braille books could be produced in large numbers. From then on, the Braille alphabet spread quickly to other countries. It was altered so that it could be used with languages where there are more or less than 26 different letters.

In this country, the telephone and recorded 'talking books' have made life more interesting for blind people, but Braille is still important. Letters and even books can be written using Braille typewriters, and computers can work in Braille too. Louis Braille's work of more than 150 years ago is still helping blind people to live fuller lives.

▲ After training, blind people read by running their fingertips quickly over the raised dots that make up the Braille alphabet. This sign is part of a nature trail for the blind at Cape Cod, Massachusetts in the United States.

▶ Using a typewriter that types raised dots on to the paper instead of letters, blind people can write a letter in Braille.

Harriet Beecher Stowe

▲ Harriet Beecher Stowe was born in 1811 and lived until 1896. Her most famous book was *Uncle Tom's Cabin*, written in 1850.

In 1776, the United States of America declared itself to be independent of Britain. The American people no longer wished to be governed by a parliament in another country. They wanted to make their own laws and to decide how to govern their country themselves. The leaders of the United States agreed that 'all men were created equal', but this was not true for black people in the United States. Most black people were slaves, which meant that they were owned by their masters. In the 50 years after the American Declaration of Independence, the northern states freed their slaves, but by 1850 there were still about four million black people living in slavery in the southern states. Some of the slaves were house servants, but most of them worked on the farms, or **plantations**. The slaves were the property of their owners and could be bought and sold as if they were cattle. If they escaped they were hunted and returned to their owners. Many slaves were treated with great cruelty.

In the northern states, people thought that all slavery should end and they tried to persuade southerners to free their slaves. One of the people who was determined that slavery should end was a writer called Harriet Beecher Stowe.

Uncle Tom's Cabin

When Harriet Beecher Stowe was 21, she moved with her family to Cincinnati in the state of Ohio. There were no slaves in Ohio, but just across the Ohio River was the state of Kentucky, where slavery still existed. In the 18 years she lived in Ohio, Beecher Stowe heard terrible stories about the lives of the slaves and the cruel way they were hunted with dogs if they escaped. She felt that she must join the fight to bring about the end of slavery.

In 1850, Harriet Beecher Stowe began to write her book, which she called *Uncle Tom's Cabin*. It told the story of a group of slaves who were to be sold. Some ran away from their plantation, and others

▲ In the southern United States, slaves were bought and sold at markets in the same way as farm animals.

were sold to new owners. *Uncle Tom's Cabin* was an exciting adventure story, so it was read by thousands of people who had never really thought about slavery before. The book was published in 1852, and 300 000 copies were sold in the first year. However, not only was it a good story, it was also a book which showed people the cruelty of slavery. It changed many people's minds, so that they too believed that the slaves should have their freedom.

Telling the truth

Many plantation owners in the southern states did not want to free their slaves. They had become wealthy because they did not pay their slaves proper wages for the work they did. These owners said that *Uncle Tom's Cabin* did not give a true picture of slaves' lives and that Harriet Beecher Stowe had made slavery sound worse than it really was in order to make a good story.

Uncle Tom's Cabin was published in Europe, and people there were shocked to find out that slavery still went on in the country that called itself 'the land of the free'. At the same time, within the United States, Harriet Beecher Stowe's book was persuading more and more people in the northern states that all slaves must be freed. The argument between the northern and southern states led to the outbreak of the American Civil War in 1861. After four years of fighting, the northern states won and slavery was ended. President Abraham Lincoln himself told Harriet Beecher Stowe that *Uncle Tom's Cabin* had helped to give the slaves their freedom.

▲ In a famous scene from *Uncle Tom's Cabin*, the slave woman Eliza escapes with her baby across a frozen river to freedom in the state of Ohio, where the slaves had been freed.

17

Julia Ward Howe

In the United States, many of the women who fought for the abolition of slavery also became interested in votes for women. The fight against slavery was a fight for equal rights, and women, like slaves, were not equal. They could not vote in **elections** so they could not take part in government. Julia Ward Howe was one of the women who believed that women should have the same rights as men. With her husband, Samuel Gridley Howe, she had supported the fight to free the slaves. When that fight had been won, she began to write and make speeches about votes for women.

▲ Julia Ward Howe became famous for her 'Battle Hymn of the Republic', which was the marching song of the northern Republican troops in the American Civil War.

The right to vote

The slaves had been given their freedom in 1865, but not the right to vote. In 1869 the United States Congress passed a law saying that all US citizens, of any race or colour, should have the right to vote, but 'citizens' still meant 'men'. Julia Ward Howe and her friends faced the task of fighting for votes for women in every single state in the country. Julia Ward Howe led the fight in the state of New England, where she lived. The women held meetings, wrote letters and gave lectures. They tried to interest other women in the fight, and organised groups in towns and villages. They kept in touch and shared ideas with women across the United States until 'votes for women' was an idea everybody heard about.

Working for peace

Julia Ward Howe worked hard for many different causes, but one that came to interest her most strongly as she grew older was world peace. In 1870 there was war in Europe between France and the former, powerful north German state of Prussia. The Prussian army swept across France and surrounded Paris. Nearly 200 000 soldiers were killed in the fighting and almost as many were wounded. When news of the war and the suffering reached the United States, Julia Ward Howe began to think of ways in which future wars could be avoided. She felt that this was something in which women could play a

◀ Groups of women in each American state got together to work for votes for women.

part. Did any woman, she asked, want to bring up sons and then watch them sent to war to be killed or wounded?

In 1872 Julia Ward Howe wrote an 'appeal to the women of the world' calling for a meeting of women to ban war. The appeal was printed in French, Spanish, Italian, German and Swedish as well as English. Julia Ward Howe travelled to Europe, in the hope of setting up a women's peace meeting, but her plans came to nothing. In the late 1800s, women's voices were not heard in the places where laws were made. Women were not taken seriously because, although they did so much important work, most men did not believe that women were able to govern. Without the vote, women had no chance of changing men's minds.

▼ Julia Ward Howe's work for women was successful, but not until ten years after her death. In 1919 women in the United States won the right to vote.

Thomas Barnardo

In London and other big cities of Europe in the mid-1800s, there were not enough houses for all the people who came to the cities to look for work. Many families had to live in a single room or even a damp and dirty cellar. People like George Peabody tried to help to provide better housing, but in London there were still thousands of homeless children who lived on the streets. Some of these children were orphans, because both their parents had died. Other children had left home because their families lived in crowded slums and there was no room for them. Children like these, who were **destitute**, made a living by doing odd-jobs, or by begging or stealing. It was a hard, dangerous and uncomfortable life, and many of the children died from cold or starvation.

Help for the homeless

In 1865 a young student, Thomas Barnardo, came to London from Dublin to train to be a doctor. His plan was to go abroad to work in China when he finished his training. In his spare time he taught at a school for poor children. One of these children told Barnardo that he was homeless, and that there were thousands like him in London. The boy, Jim Jarvis, took Barnardo through the streets of east London to see some of these children. Barnardo was horrified by what he saw and became determined to do what he could to help the homeless children of London.

Dr Barnardo and some friends began by opening a school in some old stables, where children could live as well as learn. This was soon full, and so in 1870 another, larger, home was opened in Stepney, which was one of the poorest parts of London. Dr Barnardo decided that no child in need would ever be turned away from this home, and he had a message painted along the front of the building which read: 'No destitute boy or girl ever refused admission'.

◀ The first Dr Barnardo's Home in Stepney, in London, opened in 1870.

▲ Dr Barnardo with a group of girls at the Barnardo Girls' Village, in the countryside near London.

Homes in the country

The Stepney building was the first of over 100 Dr Barnardo's Homes throughout Britain. Not all of them were built in cities. Dr Barnardo also had the idea of building children's homes in the country, away from the smoke, dirt and disease of the cities. The first of these country homes was a village for girls at Barkingside in Essex where girls lived in small 'family' groups in cottages. Each group had some adults, called **foster parents**, to look after them.

Dr Barnardo believed that it was important to give the children in his homes some kind of training for work, so that when they left the home they could earn a living. One of the homes, near the coast in Norfolk, also had a school where boys were taught skills such as sailing and how to plot a course at sea. This prepared them for a career in the navy where they would learn how to defend their country in times of war, or in the **merchant navy** where they would be taught how to trade with other countries in peacetime.

New homes, new lives

Another idea of Dr Barnardo's was to arrange for children from his homes to leave Britain to go to live with families in Canada, Australia and New Zealand. These countries welcomed young people because there were all kinds of jobs which needed to be done. Young people who moved or **emigrated** to other countries were able to start new lives there.

Dr Barnardo's Homes for children still exist today, but Barnardo's now organise many other schemes to help children and families. There are day-care centres for children with disabilities, playgroups for younger children, centres where parents can go for advice about their children, and hostels where young people who have just started work away from home can stay safely.

▼ Dr Barnardo died in 1905, after spending 40 years caring for children. In his lifetime more than 60 000 children were taken off the streets and given a home.

Henri Dunant

Until the middle of the 1800s, soldiers who were wounded in battle were usually left to look after themselves or die. There were no nurses or doctors to care for them, and there was no way of moving badly wounded men to safety. Prisoners taken by the enemy were often killed.

Today, helping the victims of war is the work of an organisation called the Red Cross. Its flag, a red cross on a white background, is known all over the world as a sign of care for the sick and wounded.

The change in attitude towards the care of wounded soldiers was brought about by one man, Henri Dunant, who was born in Geneva, Switzerland, in 1828. Dunant became a banker, and in 1859 he was in Italy on business, when he found himself in the middle of a battle between French

▼ Henri Dunant was a young businessman who dressed in fashion and enjoyed a comfortable life. What he saw at the battle of Solferino changed his life.

and Austrian troops at Solferino. The battle went on for 12 hours, and at the end 40000 soldiers lay dead or badly wounded. Dunant had never seen war before, and he was appalled by the soldiers' sufferings. He forgot about his business and walked among the wounded, doing what he could to help them. In 1862, Dunant published an account of what he had seen, called *A Memory of Solferino*. He had thought a great deal about the ways of helping people who were victims of war, and he published his ideas in the book.

The Red Cross

Dunant thought that each country should have a group of people who would travel to battlefields to look after the wounded soldiers. Many people had heard about the horrors of Solferino, and the news of the battles of the American Civil War was a reminder of the needs of war victims.

In 1864, leaders from 26 countries met in Geneva. They agreed that in time of war, wounded soldiers, people who were looking after the wounded, and hospitals, should not be thought of as enemies. They were to be called **neutral**, which would protect them from further attack.

The meeting also agreed on a mark which would be recognised by everyone. Christian countries were to use a red cross on a white background, and Muslim countries would use a red crescent. These symbols are now known all over the world, and the Red Cross is now an international organisation.

Help in trouble

▲ On 24 June 1859 about 30 000 soldiers died during the Battle of Solferino.

From that meeting in 1864, the International Red Cross grew until today it has members in almost every country. Its work grew from looking after the wounded to arranging exchanges of prisoners and helping soldiers disabled by war. The Red Cross also began giving help to the victims of peacetime disasters such as floods and earthquakes. The main centre or **headquarters** of the Red Cross are still in Geneva, but each country has its own Red Cross organisation as well.

Henri Dunant had worked hard to set up the Red Cross, but his own business failed, and by 1875 he had no money. Instead of asking his friends for help, he became a beggar and tramped around Europe finding food and shelter where he could. In 1895 a newspaper reporter met him by accident in a Swiss mountain village, living in poverty. The reporter's story reminded the world of Dunant, but he was now an old man, still haunted by the nightmare of battle. He lived on until 1910, still refusing help from his friends.

▼ Red Cross and Red Crescent flags protect doctors and nurses working on the battlefield. The sign of the Red Cross is painted on hospitals, ambulances and hospital ships in wartime.

Clara Barton

▲ Clara Barton's work for victims of war and peacetime disasters began when she was 40 years old and lasted for the rest of her long life.

The first important battle of the American Civil War was fought in July 1861 at Bull Run, a river in the state of Virginia, not far from Washington. The soldiers of both sides suffered terribly, and of the 36000 who took part in the battle, about 5000 were killed or badly wounded.

Clara Barton worked in a government office in Washington. When she heard about the battle at Bull Run she was shocked by the stories of wounded soldiers who had no bandages, drugs or other **medical supplies**. She asked the people of Washington to help, and arranged for supplies to be sent to the soldiers.

For the rest of the war, Clara Barton gave all her time to organising supplies and treatment for the wounded soldiers. It was the beginning of her life's work, caring for people who were victims of war and other disasters.

When the Civil War ended in 1865, Clara Barton turned her attention to another problem. Thousands of soldiers did not return to their homes, and no one knew whether they were dead or still alive. They were reported as missing. Clara Barton set up an office to organise searches for missing men and to find out where dead soldiers had been buried. At last, when this work was finished, she was able to take a rest. In 1869 she travelled to Europe to improve her health. It was there, in Geneva, that she first heard of the Red Cross.

The American Red Cross

Clara Barton could never rest when she knew there was work to be done, and soon she was helping with Red Cross work on the battlefields of the Franco-Prussian War. She saw how well the work was organised, and promised herself that when she returned to the United States she would start an American branch of the Red Cross.

Clara Barton returned home in 1873 and, although she was still in poor health, she began to try to persuade the United States government to accept the agreement of the rules of war called the **Geneva Convention**, and join the Red Cross. Many people in the United States thought of the Red Cross as a European organisation and wanted nothing to do with it. By 1881, 31 countries

◄ The suffering of soldiers wounded at the battle of Bull Run began Clara Barton's life's work.

Help in peace and war

Under Clara Barton's leadership, the American Red Cross grew quickly. In 1884, at a meeting in Geneva, Barton persuaded the International Red Cross to care for victims of peacetime disasters such as floods or fires as well as those who were injured by war. From then on, American Red Cross teams were ready to help wherever they could, in peacetime troubles like famines, diseases and earthquakes at home or abroad, as well as in times of war. Clara Barton continued to work full-time, and she could not be persuaded to retire until 1904, when she was 83 years old.

had their own Red Cross organisations, but the United States still did not. At last, in 1882, Congress agreed to the Geneva Convention and the American Red Cross was founded.

► Clara Barton set up field hospitals on the American Civil War battlefields. This one was at the battle of Gettysburg, in 1884.

Samuel Plimsoll

◀ The load line painted on ships today shows the level to which the ship may be loaded in different waters. TF is Tropical Fresh Water and F is Fresh Water. The lines on the right are for sea water. T is Tropical, S is Summer, W is Winter and WNA is Winter North Atlantic.

About 100 years ago, more and more goods were being carried by sea from one country to another. Shipowners were making a great deal of money by loading their ships with too many goods. They saved money by not repairing ships, so often the ships were unsafe. If the ships sank and the goods they carried, or their **cargoes**, were lost, the owners did not lose money. They paid a sum of money to an **insurance** company which agreed to pay them the cost of the ship and goods if the ship sank. The people who suffered were the seamen who drowned and their families who were left without money. Unlike the shipowners, they were not insured against disaster.

Huge numbers of ships were lost at sea. In the five years from 1864 to 1869, 10000 ships were sunk or wrecked. In one year alone, 1856, about 2300 British ships were lost.

'The sailor's friend'

One British Member of Parliament, Samuel Plimsoll, did care about the welfare of sailors and their families. He found that some shipowners were insuring their ships for far more than the ships and their cargoes were worth. The owners made more money if the ship sank than if it ended its voyage safely. The owners did not care that sailors were risking their lives. Samuel Plimsoll called these overloaded and over-insured ships 'coffin ships', because they took sailors to their deaths.

▲ Samuel Plimsoll entered Parliament with the aim of making life safer for sailors. He resigned when he decided that he could do more by working for the Seamen's Union.

In 1868, Samuel Plimsoll began to work for a change in the law to protect seamen. Many shipowners and their friends were also Members of Parliament and they fought against any change. In 1872 Plimsoll wrote a report called *Our Seamen* in which he described how sailors' lives were being put at risk. The government agreed to change the law but, at the last minute, dropped the plan because the shipowners were against it. Plimsoll, who had by this time become known as 'the sailor's friend', said that the government cared more about the money made by the shipowners than about the lives of the seamen. Many people thought Plimsoll was right. As a result the government responded to the pressure of public opinion and passed a new law in 1876 called the Merchant Shipping Act.

▶ Shipwrecks were a common sight round the coasts of Britain about 150 years ago. The *River Lune* was wrecked on the Scilly Isles, off Cornwall, in 1879. It sank in ten minutes, but luckily the crew managed to scramble to safety.

The Plimsoll line

Under the new law, government inspectors were able to go on board ships to make sure that they were fit to go to sea. A mark was painted on the side of every British ship to show how low it should be in the water when it was loaded. Other countries began to use the same mark on their own ships. The mark is still painted on ships today and is called the 'load line'. In Britain the mark is usually called 'the Plimsoll line' in memory of Samuel Plimsoll.

Plimsoll gave up, or **resigned**, his seat in Parliament, and became president of the Seamen's Union. He spent the rest of his life working for the many improvements that were needed in the way shipowners treated their sailors. These changes came slowly, but Plimsoll's first fight against overloading had saved thousands of seamen's lives and made him truly 'the sailor's friend'. Plimsoll died in 1898 but his work continued, and in 1930 an international agreement was signed by the world's major shipping countries.

Andrew Carnegie

▲ As a boy Andrew Carnegie earned just one dollar a week. When he retired in 1901, he was a millionaire.

The first railway in the United States was opened in 1829. Fifty years later, there were over 150 000 kilometres of track, crossing every state and running from the east coast to the west. There was a great deal of money to be made out of the building of railways, and Andrew Carnegie was one of the men who made it.

Carnegie was born in the Scottish town of Dunfermline. His family emigrated to the United States in 1848, when he was 13 years old. After working in a cotton mill, he joined the Pittsburgh Telegraph Company, then moved to the Pennsylvania Railroad. At the age of 24, Carnegie became a superintendant, in charge of part of the railway line.

In the 1860s, railway companies needed a great deal of iron to build their tracks, bridges and trains. Carnegie put his savings into ironworks, and his **investment** was very successful. Thirty years later in 1888, he owned eight steel companies, 700 kilometres of railway and a fleet of ships to bring supplies to his works. He was called 'the steel king of America'. When Carnegie retired in 1901 he sold his businesses for about £200 million.

The use of money

There were two sides to the character of Andrew Carnegie. He was a hard man to work for. As an **employer**, he wanted the best work for the least pay. In 1892, when workers at Homestead, one of his steelworks in Pennsylvania, asked for more money, he cut their wages instead. They went on strike, so Carnegie called in the state troops in an attempt to stop the strike.

The other side of Andrew Carnegie was the man who believed that wealth should be used to help other people. He knew that his own life would have been easier if he had had more education when he was young. So Carnegie decided to spend part of his wealth on building libraries, universities and concert halls in the United States. In Britain he also gave money for public libraries, theatres and the ballet. Whenever Carnegie gave money, he first asked the towns to give the land on which the libraries or theatres were to be built. The town councils also had to agree to look after the buildings properly. Carnegie believed strongly that people must help themselves, as well as being helped by others. He did not forget his home town of Dunfermline, where he paid for a public park, a library, a child welfare clinic and other education and welfare projects.

Man of steel

Another of Andrew Carnegie's ideas was the Carnegie Hero Fund, which he set up in the United States, Canada, Britain and other countries. The Fund gives medals and rewards to people who risk their lives to save others. He also paid for a peace school to be set up in the Netherlands. Carnegie wrote a book called *The Gospel of Wealth*, in which he said, 'The man who dies rich dies disgraced'.

Andrew Carnegie seems to have been a strange, lonely man who found it hard to form friendships with the people he knew. However, people in many countries who never met him have been helped by the wealth he made and then gave away.

▲ After the American Civil War, Andrew Carnegie started to develop the Pittsburg iron and steel industries. They were later to form the basis of the US Steel Corporation.

◄ Andrew Carnegie donated over 70 million pounds to causes in the USA and UK. He also contributed towards the building of the Carnegie Hall in New York.

Seebohm Rowntree

Some people, no matter how hard they work, never have enough money for food, clothes and a decent home. They cannot escape from poverty. This was the case for many families in Britain in the 1800s. Whilst some people lived healthier and happier lives than people had done before them, there were others who seemed to be trapped in the worst possible conditions, living miserable lives.

What was the reason? This was a question that Seebohm Rowntree asked. The Rowntrees were a wealthy family in the city of York, in northern England. There were plenty of jobs for people in York. There was a large railway works, and the Rowntree factories employed large numbers of women making sweets and chocolate. Yet even in York people lived in poverty.

Poverty in York

In 1901, Seebohm Rowntree went from house to house in the poorest areas of York, finding out how much money each family earned and how they lived. He found that one family out of every three did not have enough money to live on. One reason for this poverty was that wages were very low. Another was that there were often too many young children for the parents to look after properly. If the parents of a family became too ill to work, or died, poverty struck at once.

Rowntree found that families moved in and out of poverty according to the age of the parents. Poverty was worst when parents had young children to feed and clothe and again in old age when people could no longer work. He called this beginning and ending of life in poverty 'the **cycle** of poverty'.

One hundred years ago, there was no government help for families who were living in poverty, and none for people too

◄ A street in Leeds, England, in the 1890s. Houses like these were to be found in many British cities. The houses were badly built. They were small, dark and damp. Families who crowded in them lived in poverty and ill health.

► In Britain, medical inspection of children at school began in the 1890s. The inspections showed how sick and half-starved many poor children were.

old to work. There were no laws about how much workers should be paid. Rowntree suggested that the government should help families in poverty by paying money to people who were too sick or old to work, or were unable to get a job.

Ending the poverty trap

Rowntree published a report which described what he had found. This, and other reports on the problems which faced poor people, persuaded governments in Britain that something must be done to improve people's lives. In Germany, there was already government help for people who were too sick to work, and in New Zealand, in 1898, old people had been given an income or **pension**. In Britain, from 1908, the government began to pass laws to provide help for poor, old or sick people, although it was not until 1948 that there was some help for everyone who was living in poverty. In 1948 Britain became a 'welfare state', that is, the country decided that money should be spent on certain basic things such as free health care for everyone.

Fifty years after he wrote his first report on York, Rowntree wrote another. His 1950 report showed that one family in every 100 was still caught in the 'poverty trap'. Since 1950 there have been many changes in British laws which are meant to help people in need. Some people think that the 'welfare state' which Rowntree helped to bring about is now in danger and will not exist for very much longer.

▼ Seebohm Rowntree was chairman of his father's chocolate firm from 1925 to 1941.

Eglantyne Jebb

▲ Eglantyne Jebb grew up in a happy family in a comfortable home, and was shocked to find how many children had to live in poverty.

Eglantyne Jebb was a woman who believed that children are the most important people in the world. When children grow up, she said, they have the chance to make the world a better place than their parents made it. She believed that adults should make sure that children grow up healthy, happy and caring for each other.

After attending Oxford University, which was unusual for women in the 1890s, Jebb became a teacher. However, like many other unmarried women, when her mother fell ill, Jebb gave up her career to go home to care for her.

In 1913, Eglantyne Jebb travelled in Europe. She saw the results of war in south-east Europe, and she tried to help people who were victims of that war. She was very concerned with the sufferings of the children. A year later, the First World War began.

Children of war

The war lasted for four years. When it was over, thousands of towns and villages in Europe had been destroyed, and farm crops had been ruined. There was famine, and more than four million children were starving. Many had been separated from their families and had no hope of returning home.

Jebb, and her sister Dorothy Buxton, began collecting money to send food to fight the famine. Their first idea was to set up centres where the starving children could be fed, but the children needed more than food. There were few hospitals or clinics to treat sick children, and thousands of children had no homes. Jebb knew that people of all countries would have to work together to save the children, and that was the name she gave to the fund she set up in 1919.

Save the Children began in Britain, but within a year 40 countries had joined and more than five million pounds had been collected to help children. The money raised bought food for children in Greece, Russia, Poland and Armenia. Hospitals and schools were built and projects to help disabled children were set up.

▲ Save the Children organise vaccination programmes against polio.

Jebb saw that many problems were not caused by war itself but by poverty. Poor children's lives were often hard, their families sent them out to work and they were sometimes married or even sold without their agreement. In 1923 Jebb wrote what she called the 'Children's Charter', in which she set out children's needs for care, food and education. Some countries in Europe were working together to try to stop another war. They formed the League of Nations and the League asked Jebb to tell them how to help children. The League agreed to the 'Children's Charter' in 1924.

Save the Children today

Save the Children carries out many different kinds of welfare work for families and children in need. It is always ready to send help to places where there has been a disaster such as famine, floods or an earthquake. Families driven away from their homes by war are called **refugees**. Save the Children helps to shelter them in refugee camps until they can find a new place to settle.

Other Save the Children projects in over 50 countries now provide help for children and their families by organising health and welfare centres, playgroups, and schools for children with physical or mental handicaps. As Eglantyne Jebb said, anything can be done when 'a little love and a little money go with a well thought-out plan'.

▶ This school for children with disabilities is in Morocco. It is run by Save the Children.

Helen Keller

Helen Keller was born in 1880 in a small town in Alabama in the United States. She was a healthy, happy baby until, when she was 19 months old, illness struck her. 'Suddenly I was raised into a bright light. I felt a great pain which made me scream.' This was how Helen Keller remembered the moment when she went blind and deaf.

Helen had just started to talk, but because she could no longer hear words she could not learn to say them. Her parents did not know how to help her. They could not even make her know that they were there, except by touching her. This was the only way they could **communicate** with Helen.

As Helen grew older, her parents became more and more worried. When they did not understand what she wanted, she kicked and screamed and threw things about. Helen's parents heard about a school in Boston which tried to help blind people. They asked the school to help Helen, and in 1887, 25-year-old Annie Sullivan came to teach Helen.

Annie Sullivan

Annie herself had been born nearly blind, so she understood the problems of blind children. At first, Helen behaved as badly with Annie as she had done with her parents, but slowly Annie made friends with her. Annie began to teach Helen words by spelling them letter by letter on the palm of Helen's hand. Helen learned to 'hear' words by placing the tips of her fingers on Annie's throat and feeling the movements. By the age of ten Helen Keller had learned to speak.

Now that Helen could make herself understood and understand others, she learnt very quickly. When she was 20, she went to Radcliffe, the women's college of Harvard University. With Annie sitting beside her to spell out what the lecturers were saying, Helen became one of the best students of her year. When she left Radcliffe she knew four languages and had written a book about the first 20 years of her life, which she called *The Story of my Life*.

◄ Annie Sullivan spelling out words for Helen Keller.

Helping others

Helen Keller's blindness and deafness gave her a special understanding of other people with disabilities. After *The Story of my Life* was published, many people asked Helen how they could help blind people. Helen knew that more schools were needed for blind children and that money must be found to build and staff them. She also knew that people must stop thinking that blind people cannot live ordinary lives. Helen Keller helped to achieve these aims by writing appeals to raise money and by advising teachers on the needs of blind children. Blind adults, too, needed special training so that they could earn a living for themselves. Helen travelled all over the United States and Europe, lecturing on the problems which blind people faced and explaining how blind people wished to be treated. Most important of all, Helen Keller's life, which ended in 1968, showed people with disabilities, and those who wanted to help them, that they could live their own lives and have a place in the world like anyone else.

▲ Helen Keller at work in her study in 1902.

▼ In February 1955, Helen Keller, aged 70, visited London for three days during a world tour. Beside her is her translator companion.

Albert Schweitzer

▲ Albert Schweitzer was educated at the universities of Strasbourg, Paris and Berlin. He had doctorates in philosophy, theology and music as well as medicine and surgery. He was also a gifted musician.

Albert Schweitzer was born in 1876 in Alsace, an area which is now in France but was then a part of Germany. When Schweitzer was 21 he was a student at Strasbourg University, training to become a **minister** of the Lutheran Church. He was also studying music. Some people plan their lives carefully, and others wait to see what happens to them. While he was still a student, Albert Schweitzer made a plan for his life. He decided that when he was 30 he would give all his time and energy to helping others. Schweitzer told no one about this plan, but went on working hard and in 1903 he became a college professor.

At about this time, Schweitzer read a magazine article about the need for doctors in Africa. This, he decided, was what he would do with his life. He would study to be a doctor, and go to work in Africa.

Forest doctor

Albert Schweitzer finished his training to become a doctor in 1911. In the next year he married, and began to plan the journey to Africa. His wife shared his ideas about caring for people. She was a **scholar** and studied at the university, but she retrained as a nurse so that she could share the work in Africa. Early in 1913 the Schweitzers set out for the state of Gabon, which was then part of the French empire in West Africa, to build a hospital in the village of Lambaréné.

Lambaréné is in one of the hottest parts of Africa, on the Equator. It is surrounded by forests, and for most of the year the weather is thundery and damp, which makes any kind of work very tiring. There was more than enough work for the Schweitzers. There were **tropical diseases** to be treated, injuries to be bandaged, operations to be carried out and babies to be looked after. In the first nine months, 2000 patients were treated by the Schweitzers.

▲ Albert Schweitzer with a patient at Lambaréné.

In the evenings, after his day's work, Schweitzer would read, write or play the organ. On Sundays he held a church service. Schweitzer believed that every living thing has a right to life, and he taught people to have what he called 'a reverence for life'.

▼ Albert Schweitzer worked at Lambaréné to the end of his life. He died, aged 90, in 1965 and was buried at Lambaréné, the place which had been his home for over 50 years.

Travels abroad

Albert Schweitzer's work at Lambaréné could not go on without money for medical supplies and equipment. About every two years, Schweitzer returned to Europe to give lectures and organ concerts to raise money for the work in Africa. The money he made from these journeys was enough to build a new, modern hospital at Lambaréné.

In 1952, Albert Schweitzer was awarded the Nobel Peace Prize, which is given every year to people whose work helps towards peace in the world. With this money he decided to build a village for people who suffered from leprosy, the tropical disease which rots away the body. The village was built near the hospital.

Schweitzer went on working at Lambaréné to the end of his life. He died aged 90, in 1965 and was buried, as he had asked, at Lambaréné, the place which had been his home for over 50 years.

Mother Teresa

◀ Mother Teresa believes that showing people love and care is as important as doing things for them.

The slums of Calcutta, in India, are some of the worst in the world. Thousands of people live in homes made of scraps of wood and plastic. Thousands more live on the streets, finding shelter wherever they can. Many people are starving, sick and homeless. Children are often left to look after themselves because there is no one to care for them.

In 1948, a Christian nun called Sister Teresa went to live in the Calcutta slums. She believed that God had told her to spend the rest of her life helping the people there and living alongside them.

She changed her nun's clothes for the simple cotton robe worn by Indian women, which is called a sari.

Sister Teresa's move to the slums changed her life completely. Born in part of Albania, which is now in Yugoslavia, Sister Teresa had lived in India for nearly 20 years, but had spent that time teaching in church schools at the convents where the nuns lived. She had little knowledge of life outside. She was 38 years old, and the great work of her life was about to begin.

Helping people in need

The first thing Sister Teresa did was to start a school. It was held in the open air, and she taught by scratching words in the sand as she had no blackboard or paper. When she was not teaching, she went about collecting food, money and medicines to give to people who had none. Some of the girls Sister Teresa had taught in the convent heard about her work and came to join her, and a friend let her use part of his house for a school.

In 1950 the Pope allowed Sister Teresa to start a new group, or **order**, of nuns which

▼ The work that Mother Teresa began in 1948 will continue for as long as it is needed.

▲ Mother Teresa began to work with children, but her work spread to include the old, the sick, the dying, the homeless and drug addicts.

she called the Missionaries of Charity. She was head of the order and became Mother Teresa. Nuns who joined the order promised to spend their lives helping 'the poorest of the poor'. The nuns were allowed to own nothing except their clothes and a prayer book.

The Missionaries of Charity continued to work in Calcutta among the people in need. Soon, there were schools, children's homes, clinics, hospitals and special places called hospices where people who are dying can spend their last days in peace.

World fame

As news of Mother Teresa's work spread, many people sent money to help her and others came to work with her. The order grew and its work spread throughout India and into other countries. Now, the Missionaries of Charity work in more than 300 places in over 70 countries.

Mother Teresa is known and loved all over the world. In 1979 she was awarded the Nobel Peace Prize. When she went to Sweden to receive her prize, she said, 'I accept the prize in the name of the poor. By serving the poor I am serving Jesus.'

Martin Luther King

In 1863, the last of the black slaves in the United States were set free. However, although black Americans were free, they were not treated like other Americans. In 1955, over 90 years later, they still had the lowest-paid jobs and the worst housing, and they were less healthy and less well-educated than white people. In the southern states, black people were not allowed to use the same schools, shops, churches, libraries or even parks as white people. In cinemas, theatres and on buses they had to sit separately. Today, in South Africa, this system of separating black people from white people still exists. There, the system of keeping people apart is called **apartheid**.

In the United States, some black people wanted to use force to gain equal rights, but one black leader believed that his people should protest in **non-violent** ways. He was Martin Luther King, a church minister from Montgomery in the southern state of Alabama.

Black protest

On 1 December, 1955, Rosa Parks, a black shop worker, caught a bus home after her day's work in Montgomery. There was one seat left, and she sat on it. When some white people boarded the bus and one person had to stand, he ordered Rosa Parks to give up her seat. She refused, so the police were called, and Rosa Parks was arrested.

This led to the start of the black Americans' non-violent protest. Martin Luther King was amongst the people who refused to use the buses because of Rosa Parks' treatment. King's home was bombed, and white people in Montgomery began to attack blacks. King urged black people to keep up their **boycott** and refuse to use the buses, but not to attack white people. A year later the bus company agreed to allow black people equal rights on the buses.

◀ Martin Luther King after the Washington protest march in August 1963. His 'I have a dream' speech made him world-famous, and in 1964 he was awarded the Nobel Peace Prize.

▲ Black people in Montgomery, Alabama, kept up their bus boycott for over a year until in December 1956, the US government ordered that the separation of black and white people on buses must end.

After this, Martin Luther King became the leader of the movement to win equal **civil rights** for all black people. Black students organised **sit-ins** at places where whites would not serve them. They sat down and refused to move. These non-violent protests were met with beatings and bombings from white people in the southern states. Martin Luther King was jailed several times. Newspapers and television around the world began to take an interest in what was happening, and their stories and films made many white Americans ashamed of their country.

'I have a dream'

In August 1963 it was 100 years since the slaves had been set free, and a march was organised in Washington, the capital of the United States. It was a peaceful march, with 250 000 people taking part. Martin Luther King marched with them. Later, he spoke to the crowd. 'I have a dream', he said, 'that my four little children will one day live in a nation where they will not be judged by the colour of their skin.' Only then, he added, the United States could truly call itself 'the land of the free'. In 1964, Martin Luther King's work towards achieving equal rights for black people earned him the Nobel Peace Prize. However, Martin Luther King never saw his dream of equality come true. In 1968, speaking after a march for equal pay for blacks and whites, in Memphis, Tennessee, he was shot and killed.

Black people in the United States are still not always treated equally, but thanks to Martin Luther King some of the barriers between black and white have been removed.

▼ Martin Luther King at the head of a civil rights march. Jail, the bombing of his home and threats on his life did not deter him from his aim of equal rights for his people.

Desmond Tutu

▲ Archbishop Tutu prays for the day when black and white South Africans can live together freely and as equals.

Desmond Tutu has one of the most difficult jobs in the world. He is Archbishop of the Anglican Church in South Africa. This means that he is the leader of millions of South African Christians, both black and white, in a country where the lives of blacks and whites are separated by the laws of apartheid.

Under apartheid, not only are blacks and whites separated but white people have better access to jobs and land than black people, and most of the laws are made by an exclusively white government. In addition, black people suffer by not being permitted to own land, to move freely and to live where they would like to live.

As a person born and brought up in South Africa, Desmond Tutu loves the country but hates the way it is being torn apart by the divisions and conflicts between black and white people. He believes it is his duty to try and make South Africa a place where all people, black or white, can be happy and live alongside one another.

Teacher and preacher

As a child Desmond Tutu wanted to become a doctor, but his family could not afford the cost of the long training. He studied at a teachers' training college instead. When he started teaching in a school for black children, he found that they were taught only enough to enable them to do the poorest-paid work. This angered Tutu so much that he left, and began to train as a minister of the Anglican Church.

▲ Thousands of black people live in the all-black suburb of Soweto, outside Johannesburg, and many live in very poor conditions. Blacks may not buy houses in the white residential areas.

Tutu went to London to study. This was his first journey outside South Africa and he and his wife were amazed to find out what it was like to live in a country where black people are as free as white. 'We didn't need to carry passes,' he remembers. 'We didn't have to look for signs telling us whether we could be where we were.'

'We will be free'

Tutu's work as a bishop, where he preached peace and justice between black and white people in South Africa, earned him the Nobel Peace Prize in 1984. Two years later, he became Archbishop of Cape Town.

There are many white people in South Africa who believe that everyone should have equal rights, and Archbishop Tutu is confident about this. 'We are going to be free,' he says. 'About that there is no doubt. We ask only *How?* and *When?*' Even though the South African government is negotiating with black political parties, Tutu fears that if change does not happen soon black people will bring about change themselves, but through violence. As a Christian, Tutu is opposed to violence as a way of changing the system. Instead he has asked the governments of other countries to refuse to trade with South Africa until all South Africans are free and equal.

▶ As head of the Anglican Church in South Africa, Archbishop Tutu works for peace and justice and an end to apartheid.

Time chart

Date	Europe, Australia, New Zealand	Asia	Africa	North, Central and South America
1769	Johann Pestalozzi opens his first school at Yverdon, in Switzerland			
1776				The American colonies declare their independence from Britain
1791	Philippe Pinel publishes his report on mental patients in France			
1801	Pestalozzi publishes his book on teaching, called *How Gertrude teaches her children*			
1813	Elizabeth Fry's first visit to Newgate Prison			
1829	Louis Braille publishes the first version of his alphabet			The first railway is opened in the United States
1852				Harriet Beecher Stowe publishes *Uncle Tom's Cabin*
1854	Louis Braille's alphabet taught to blind people in France			
1861-1865				The American Civil War
1862	The first Peabody Dwellings are built in London Henri Dunant publishes *A Memory of Solferino*			
1864	The first meeting of the International Red Cross takes place in Geneva, Switzerland			
1869				The United States Congress passes a law giving all male citizens the right to vote
1870	The first Dr Barnardo's Home is opened in Stepney, London			
1872	Samuel Plimsoll writes his report on ships and shipping, *Our Seamen*			Julia Ward Howe makes her appeal to women for world peace
1876	The British Parliament passes the Merchant Shipping Act, and the 'Plimsoll Line' is introduced			
1882				The United States signs the Geneva Convention and the American Red Cross is founded. Clara Barton is its first President
1887				Annie Sullivan becomes Helen Keller's teacher

Date	Europe, Australia, New Zealand	Asia	Africa	North, Central and South America
1901	Seebohm Rowntree publishes his first study of poverty in York, England			
1904				Clara Barton resigns as President of the American Red Cross
1913			Albert Schweitzer goes to Lambaréné for the first time	
1919				Women in the United States are given the right to vote
1920	Save the Children becomes an international fund			
1923	Eglantyne Jebb writes the 'Children's Charter'			
1948	Britain's National Health Service begins			
1950	Seebohm Rowntree writes his last report on poverty in York, England	The Missionaries of Charity are founded with Mother Teresa as head		
1952			Albert Schweitzer is awarded the Nobel Peace Prize	
1955				Non-violent protests by black Americans begin in Alabama, in the United States
1963				Martin Luther King makes his famous speech, 'I have a dream'
1964				Martin Luther King receives the Nobel Peace Prize
1968				Martin Luther King is shot dead in Memphis, Tennessee, in the United States
1979		Mother Teresa is awarded the Nobel Peace Prize		
1984			Desmond Tutu is awarded the Nobel Peace Prize	
1986			Desmond Tutu becomes Archbishop of Cape Town	

Glossary

apartheid: the government-controlled system in South Africa which separates black people from white people

asylum: a hospital for people who are mentally ill

boycott: to refuse to have anything to do with someone or something as a means of showing disapproval

cargo: the goods which are carried by a ship or a plane

charity: an organisation which collects money and uses it to help people

civil rights: the rights of the people of a particular country which are recognised by the laws of that country. In some countries today people have no civil rights which means, for example, that they cannot take part in choosing the government or the ruler of their country

communicate: to pass ideas and information on to other people by means of speech, writing or in some other way

cycle: a set of events which repeat themselves in a regular pattern

destitute: describes people who are homeless and have no way of earning a living

election: the selection of a person or a political party by a group of voters

emigrate: to leave one country to go to live in another country

employer: a person or a business which pays other people to work for them

famine: a time when there is little or no food or water in a country or region because of a disaster like a bad drought

foster parents: people who look after a child while his or her own parents are unable to do so

found: to set up an organisation, institution or business

Geneva Convention: the international agreement which was made in Geneva, Switzerland in 1864. The Geneva Convention set up a series of rules which dealt with the treatment of sick and wounded soldiers. Later conventions covered subjects such as warfare at sea and treatment of prisoners of war

headquarters: the main office of a business or organisation

Hinduism: the religion which is based on more than one god and a belief in re-birth. Hindus believe that the way people live one life affects the sort of life they will be re-born into

humanitarian: a person who cares about the welfare of other people

insurance: an arrangement by which a person pays money to a firm. If something goes wrong, the firm agrees to pay that person money. For example, a health insurance firm pays a patient's bill at a private hospital

investment: the act of putting money into a business in the hope that the business will be successful and make a profit for the investor

Islam: the religion which is based on the teachings of the Prophet Mohammed. Followers of Islam are called Muslims

leprosy: a disease which affects the skin and nerves and which slowly rots the whole body

medical supplies: equipment and medicines which are used to treat sick people

mentally ill: describes someone who is suffering from sickness of the mind

merchant: a person who buys and sells goods, often travelling to other countries to do business

merchant navy: ships and their crews which carry goods or transport passengers

minister: a Christian who takes church services and teaches about God

neutral: not supporting any country or group of countries during a war, but remaining independent instead

non-violent: a way of protesting which does not involve using weapons or physical force

order: a community of religious people, such as nuns or monks, who live together and follow certain rules about how to live

pension: a regular payment which is made to someone who is old or ill and cannot earn their own living

plantation: a large area of land where one type of plant or tree is grown. Coffee, rubber and tea are grown on plantations

refugee: a person who has to leave their home and often their own country to escape from war

resign: to give up a job or a post within an organisation

sanitation: the system of providing water and disposing of sewage safely from buildings which helps to keep people in good health

scholar: a person who spends time studying and learning

sit-in: a form of protest where people sit down in a public place and refuse to move

slum housing: houses which provide inadequate living conditions by being dirty, overcrowded and without proper sanitation

tax: a payment which the people of a country must make to their government. Taxes pay for the running of the government and all the services that it provides

tropical disease: an illness which occurs in the tropics. The tropics are the very hot, damp regions of the Earth which are found near the Equator

Index